PRIVATE GARDENS OF
THE BAY AREA

PRIVATE GARDENS OF
THE BAY AREA

Susan Lowry and Nancy Berner

Photographs by Marion Brenner

THE MONACELLI PRESS

THE PENINSULA

SAN FRANCISCO

Frontispiece: Aloe polyphylla, Yucca linearifolia, and
Alcanterea 'Julietta' in mixed planting in front of Ann
Nichols's house in Berkeley.
Pages 42–43: An armillary sphere is framed by Swan Hill
fruitless olives, Iceberg roses, and Euphorbia 'Blue Haze' in
Karen and Ned Gilhuly's garden in Woodside.
Pages 78–79: Cliff House on Telegraph Hill overlooking the
waterfront, with the Bay Bridge in the distance.
Pages 120–21: Fantastical planting in Vera and John Pardee's
Berkeley garden.
Pages 162–63: View from Molly Chappellet's garden over the
vineyard to Lake Hennessey.

EAST BAY

MARIN
SONOMA
NAPA

INTRODUCTION

In garden design, the borrowed landscape is a long-cherished ideal. In the San Francisco Bay Area, the breadth of the sky, the quality of the light, the sparkle of the Bay, the shapes of the hills are all part of the narrative that any successful Bay Area garden needs to engage. Gardens also need to engage complicated microclimates, frequent drought, and the heterogeneous cultural factors at work there. The kaleidoscope of vigorous plants from five continents bursting out of an Oakland front yard is one kind of California garden, the clean-lined contemporary composition of drought-tolerant natives and gravel is another, and the garden tucked into the mountain landscape of oaks, manzanitas, and ceanothus is yet another. Linking them together is the energetic interplay between a rich and varied design vocabulary and an open embrace of the magnificent natural setting.

Before we embarked on this project, we had looked enviously at the Bay Area as a region of spectacular scenic beauty that also seemed to be a gardener's paradise, with no off-season and the possibility of growing almost anything a plant lover's heart might desire. When we started to explore, we had a superb guide in our good friend Marion Brenner. In fact, the reason we even dared to attempt such a project was that Marion, a passionate gardener herself, has been recording California gardens and landscapes in books and magazines for over twenty years. We relied on her encyclopedic knowledge to find the best examples in the Bay Area. What followed were multiple trips over almost two years that altogether became a road trip extraordinaire. We visited more than one hundred gardens and talked constantly about style, plants, history, designers, and what exactly defines a "California Garden," expanding and refining our definition along the way. It was immediately clear that there is no one California voice but a multitude of styles and voices, and we chose to celebrate the diversity of approaches we found, which reflect the geography of the region and its myriad microclimates. All three of us were particularly drawn to gardens that were personal statements, where their owners and/or makers were totally committed to them, and those became the focus of our study.

Sustainability was a constant topic of conversation. There was a general agreement among professionals and amateurs alike that drought or no drought, gardens and garden design are increasingly influenced by environmental issues.

Donnell Garden, designed in 1948 by Thomas Church.

Although no gardener was willing to give up having a garden in periods of extreme drought, each one had developed strategies to cope—in some cases, reducing lawn areas, in others substituting drought-tolerant plants.

In fact, the question of water has always had to be uppermost in California gardeners' minds. The earliest gardening was done at the missions. Spain had claimed what is now the state of California in 1542, but there was no attempt to settle the area until 1769 when missionaries set out from Mexico to convert the native population. Early Spanish missions were based loosely on those of Andalusia, which had a similarly Mediterranean climate and where many of the explorers and missionaries originated. The gardens of Andalusia were in turn based on the Islamic paradise garden with its sophisticated and conservative use of water. The padres introduced useful plants that would provide food, wine, and medicine for the community and decoration for the church. Oranges and lemons, olives, and grape vines all came to California with the missions. A fruit tree is still an almost universal attribute of the California garden, from productive kitchen gardens to the most elegant city parterre. After the missions were dissolved by Mexico in 1834, in an effort to encourage settlers and the development of civilian communities, Mexican authorities granted huge tracts of land to individuals, and settlers from the United States and Europe started to move into the sparsely settled territory.

By 1847 the American acquisition of California was complete. In 1848 gold was discovered, a year later the Gold Rush began in earnest, and in 1850 California became a state. A tidal wave of people made the arduous journey to California,

Arizona Garden, Stanford
University campus.

and with them myriad cultures, ideas, and attitudes swept over the state. The
myth of California as a land of plenty, where anything was possible, took hold.
As historian David C. Streatfield wrote in *California Gardens: Creating a New
Eden*: "Whatever their subsequent failings as managers, the Spanish followed
principles for living in a semiarid climate that were appropriate and that, with
few exceptions, were totally ignored by later American settlers."

Settlers arrived in California with their own set of aesthetics and traditions
and looked to replicate them, often on a grander scale. Almost immediately, the
newly rich built huge estates, based on what they knew of European, mostly
Victorian, models. Sweeping lawns, which had come into fashion in part thanks
to the widely disseminated works of A. J. Downing, were an important part
of this Romantic ideal. In California, given the climate and soil conditions and
dazzled by the horticultural opportunities, gardeners could grow a wide range
of plants to perfection—with the addition of water—often producing floral
profusion of an intensity unknown in the region and style of origin. Exuberance
seems to have been the watchword of these early garden makers, who often
went to great lengths in the dry climate to secure the water rights to enable
them to make their gardens.

The Victorian addiction to plant collecting was shared by these early garden
owners. It was made all the more attractive because the possibilities seemed
endless. Leland Stanford's cactus collection, originally put together by Rudolf
Ulrich in 1887 as an "Arizona Garden," still graces the Stanford campus. In the

spirit of importing garden styles the way one would collect any other possession, Japanese gardens became all the rage after the California International Midwinter Exposition, held in San Francisco in 1894. The Japanese Garden designed by Makoto Hagiwara and installed for that event is still one of the main attractions of Golden Gate Park, and it inspired a number of private efforts. The earliest of these, Higurashi-en, also designed by Hagiwara, still exists in private hands in Hillsborough. To this day, we see gardeners creating classically composed Japanese gardens, although the subtle influence of Japanese Zen gardens has been more significant in contemporary landscape design.

Even in the earliest, most frenetic days of the state, there were voices advocating or practicing a more restrained form of garden creation, predicated on sound environmental practice. In his design for Stanford University in the 1880s, Frederick Law Olmsted searched for indigenous historical precedents and planted the quads with drought-tolerant plants. William Hammond Hall, who laid out Golden Gate Park and became its first superintendent, did so with ecological principles in mind. Aesthetically, some strove for a naturalistic look, as did John McLaren who followed Hall as superintendent and stayed in the post for over fifty years. But McLaren also enthusiastically used the widest possible plant palette and was proud that the park featured trees from across the world. The architect Bernard Maybeck, in his work with the Hillside Club in the Berkeley hills, advocated lush but naturalistic planting to complement his arts-and-crafts–inspired homes.

Left: Higurashi-en, Hillsborough.

Right: Bernard Maybeck house, Berkeley.

Left: Alcatraz Island.

Right: Filoli, Woodside.

The gardens of the early tycoons were laid out by professionals, initially nurserymen, later joined by landscape designers or architects. Professional designers continue to play an outsized role in California garden-making. In this climate, creating a well-designed garden is almost like adding another room to the house. The observation that "gardens are for people," coined by San Francisco landscape architect Thomas Church and the title of his 1955 book, has real validity in a place that is comfortable outside almost year round and where the outdoor space flows directly from the indoor space. Church himself, many of whose gardens are still extant in the Bay Area, was part of a generation of influential practitioners that included the landscape architect Garret Eckbo and architect Richard Neutra, who made the ideas of California modernism part of an international design vocabulary. The Western lifestyle had no bigger proponent than Sunset Publishing, whose magazine (first published in 1898), books, and demonstration gardens have taught generations of Westerners about appropriate styles and plants for the California landscape. California gardens remain on the cutting edge of design, both in public and private spheres.

The nursery trade has also been very influential. By the mid-1850s, nurseries were importing seeds and plants from as far away as Australia and were soon using their ever-expanding stocks to create the showy estates of the early moguls. In our day, Western Hills, the legendary nursery in Occidental that provided plants and expertise to a wide range of connoisseurs, also produced garden designers such as Roger Warner. Annie's Annuals in Richmond and Flora Grubb Gardens in southeast San Francisco offer an extensive palette of new plant introductions and also new directions in garden design.

We have chosen to focus on private gardens because the Bay Area's exceptional and highly influential public gardens are for the most part well documented. However, they were an essential part of our understanding of the region. Two botanical gardens—the San Francisco and the UC/Berkeley—are significant resources for education, whether about native plants or a wider palette made possible by the climate, and the small and focused Quarry Hill in Glen Ellen has an important collection of wild-collected Asian plants. An eclectic mix of historical and contemporary gardens both preserve history and further expand the public's understanding of plants.

By far the grandest garden open to the public is Filoli in Woodside, designed by Bruce Porter beginning in 1917 for Mr. and Mrs. William Bowers Bourn, a prominent San Francisco family. Its carefully articulated, intimate garden rooms set against the backdrop of the Santa Cruz Mountains remain an iconic representation of the elegance and aspiration of the era. The gardens on Alcatraz Island in San Francisco Bay, visited by over a million tourists annually, have been sensitively restored over a number of years through an unusual partnership between The Garden Conservancy and the Golden Gate National Parks Conservancy. Scores of volunteers take the early ferry weekly to continue the work of rehabilitating the historic landscape, first planted by the military officers and families and prison inmates who lived on the rocky island. The stunning cactus and succulent collections at the Ruth Bancroft Garden in Walnut Creek expand our definitions of what is beautiful and what is possible to grow successfully in the Bay Area and also celebrate its remarkable founder, still living on the property in her 108th year. The Marin Art & Garden

Left: Ruth Bancroft Garden, Walnut Creek.

Right: Western Hills Garden, Occidental.

Center in Ross is a community resource that complements its garden setting with extensive programming in the arts. In Sonoma, Cornerstone Gardens showcases the work of contemporary landscape architects and designers in a series of garden installations and is also the home of the newly installed Sunset demonstration gardens, designed by Homestead Garden Collective.

Given the diversity of style, landscape, and climate in the Bay Area, we chose to group the gardens in this book geographically because, while there are stylistic variations, the similarities of light, landscape, climate, and density in each section's gardens offered an organizing principle. We began on the Peninsula, where the Santa Cruz Mountains block the fog that makes the city of San Francisco cool and damp in the summer months, so the interior valley is almost invariably sunny and warm, especially in the summer. Here, the gentle landscape, wooded hills, and long garden tradition—and now also the close proximity to Silicon Valley—have created a rich matrix for gardenmaking. In the nineteenth century, wealthy San Franciscans took advantage of the climate and established enormous and extravagant estates, which have been broken up over time into much smaller properties and suburbs. The gardens in the more sparsely populated mountains retain their rural ambience and wide views.

In the densely packed city of San Francisco, the range of styles and gardens is astonishing despite its challenging microclimates and the fog and wind. The city's distinctive staircase gardens and small back yards, often steeply rising or falling, display traditional elegance, innovative spatial organization, engineering know-how and avant-garde landscaping. The technical issues seem to have provoked the talented designers of the city to do some of their best and most idiosyncratic work. Looking at the varied approaches to these often-tiny gardens bears out the truth of landscape architect Ron Lutsko's observation that inventiveness is the key ingredient in Bay Area gardens.

The East Bay section is dominated by gardens in the cities of Oakland and Berkeley, where the ebullience and plantsmanship of front yards is infectious. Here, almost twenty years ago, an informal group of plant enthusiasts dubbed themselves the Hortisexuals and started a movement that continues today. They filled their gardens with the most interesting plants they could discover as they traveled the world, knitting their various finds together in intense and lush plant-focused creations that they delight in displaying to their neighbors and the public. So, while we have included some large gardens in the warmer hills inland from the Bay, we focused on these imaginative and downright joyful plant collections displayed in front of often modest homes.

Marin, Napa, and Sonoma counties are considered together. Marin's agricultural past may have morphed into expensive suburbs, but it also includes great swaths of scenic landscape that have been preserved by forward-thinking local conservationists. Marin includes the hillsides of Tiburon above the Bay, with its spectacular views and gardens carefully composed to take advantage of them, as well as older communities like Ross, whose gardens are often burnished with the patina of age and tradition. In Napa and Sonoma, the two mountain ranges provide outlooks and the flat plains in between allow long views of the kind of agriculture that built the economy of California. Because this is real agricultural production, the gardens in the wine country acknowledge their landscape very directly, especially those attached to vineyards. The more rustic gardens in the hills and mountains above strive to balance design with the enormous views and the native landscape.

Finally, a word about our choices. The Bay Area has a huge number of remarkable gardens and we could have filled not just one book but several volumes with superb examples. The selections that follow were chosen by the three of us for excellence certainly, but also with an eye to demonstrating the multiplicity of voices that take advantage of the particular conditions of soil, climate, and landscape that make gardeners all over the world wish they could garden here.

Frances Bowes Garden, Sonoma.

THE PENINSULA

GREEN GABLES

WOODSIDE

In the second half of the nineteenth century, wealthy San Franciscans began to build large estates on the Peninsula to escape the cold summer fog of the city. After the San Francisco earthquake in 1906, prominent businessman and philanthropist Mortimer Fleishhacker followed suit, choosing to build in Woodside, where he eventually acquired seventy-five acres of land with long views south and west to the Santa Cruz Mountains. For over one hundred years, the Fleishhacker family has spent their summers at Green Gables, enjoying the privacy that this unique setting provides.

The rambling house and extensive grounds were designed in 1911 by Charles Greene, of Greene and Greene, the preeminent American practitioners of the arts and crafts style. The Fleishhackers wanted an English house with a thatched roof, and Greene gave them a California interpretation, using gunite (a form of concrete, invented in 1907, that can be sprayed onto walls) to construct the light beige walls and Pacific redwood shakes, steamed and molded, to simulate thatching. The gardens were built in stages, beginning with the brick terraces and sloping lawn in back of the house. Gravel paths lead down the lawn and terminate in a lower brick terrace with a T-shaped lily pool. Specimen trees were planted, including the now-venerable Blue Atlas Cedars to the side of the house. The only flower gardens were along the upper terrace. Over time, the Fleishhackers felt that the garden wasn't complete, and they brought Greene back in 1927.

Greene's inspired solution was a great reveal that can be seen only from the terrace at the far side of the lily pool. There, a double set of stone steps leads down on either side of a succulent and perennial garden to a dramatic 300-foot-long pool that evokes a Roman ruin. Below the stairs is a grotto and, on the far side, an arcade reminiscent of a Roman aqueduct whose arches are both reflected in the water and also lead the eye out to the landscape beyond. Handsome green-glazed ceramic pots, designed by Greene for the site, are set on top of the arches and also, filled with white oleanders, line the gravel pathways on either side of

Above: Greene used fieldstone and flagstone for paths and steps and pieces of red chirt to form these large urns.

Opposite: A double staircase sweeps down four hundred feet to the blind arcade and the Roman pool.

Overleaf: The dramatic Roman pool is the centerpiece of the garden.

the pool. Greene's masterful use of stone in the pool, the staircase, the balustrade,
and the terraces, as well as in many of the planting urns—he used mostly local
fieldstone and rough, dark-red bricks, with red chirt for accents—illustrate his
articulation of every aspect of the garden.

Today, the garden is close to the archival images from one hundred years ago.
The mature trees have reached impressive proportions, yet the balance in the
landscape remains perfect. And, most importantly, the patina of age has only
enhanced Greene's masterpiece.

Above: Wisteria is draped over the arches at the far end of the reflecting pool. Glazed pots, designed by Charles Greene, line the paths and dot the top of the arcade.

Opposite: An allée of venerable Camperdown elms.

A PENINSULA GARDEN

At once grand and romantic, this landscape designed by landscape architect Lawrence Halprin has a unique voice. It combines many of the elements of a classically inspired garden with a more muscular vision informed by Halprin's modernist sensibility, and it also illustrates how a skillful use of water can add depth and meaning.

In his later years, Halprin very rarely took on private commissions, but the owners, captivated by a number of his public projects, persuaded him to design their garden. At first glance, the many traditional elements in this estate, which were inspired by the owner's European travels, seem at odds with Halprin's usual spare but forceful approach, but, as he said of himself, "Modernism, as I define it and practice it, includes and is based on the vital archetypal needs of human beings as individuals as well as social groups."

The owners bought the five-acre property in 1986, and the house and garden were designed a few years later, with the owners as the lynchpin between the architect, Ugo Sap, and the landscape architect, ensuring a unified vision. When it came to the garden, the owners had a list of elements they wanted Halprin to address: water features, a lawn for children to play football and baseball, and also a secret garden and a decorative but productive vegetable and flower garden. In addition to the specific elements, on a broader level they wanted a verdant, finished landscape.

Off the entrance courtyard, an unobtrusive door leads to the walled secret garden, built from a mixture of cut limestone and natural stone, with a discreet rill incised into the paving. The other garden rooms are located behind the house, in a complex that includes the terrace and pool, tennis court, flower garden, knot garden, and potager and some of the seventy-two fruit trees on the property. Tall hedges of cherry laurel enclose each garden area. The cutting garden provides flowers for the house, and the formal potager, with its organically grown vegetables in perfect formation springing from specially

Above: Steps descend from the terrace to the lawn below.

Opposite: Halprin designed this powerful waterfall tumbling down the hillside into a small lake. Pineapple guavas (*Feijoa sellowiana*), escallonia, loropetalum and mugo pines nestle into the hillside beside it, and a shapely live oak (*Quercus agrifolia*) grows on the island.

Overleaf: The slope below the house is covered with Asiatic jasmine (*Trachelospermum asiaticum*), which both helps prevent erosion and provides textural contrast. Special care was taken to preserve the existing oaks on the hillside.

Above: All the annuals, perennials, shrubs, and trees in the secret garden sport white flowers. Here, a seasonal display of hydrangea, agapanthus, alyssum, and impatiens.

Opposite above: Tall, glossy cherry laurel hedges (*Prunus caroliniana* 'Bright and Tight') delineate garden rooms near the house.

Opposite below: Vegetables for the kitchen are neatly laid out in decorative raised beds.

Above: Water trickles down
the rough-hewn central panel
of the pergola wall, which
is softened by the oakleaf
hydrangea (*Hydrangea quercifolia*) draping over it.

Opposite: A substantial wiste-
ria-covered pergola stands at
a high point of the property
to take advantage of views,
especially the sunset.

designed boxes, provides ample produce in the years of adequate rain. In the
pool terrace adjacent to the house, a dramatic cascade roars down wide steps
into the shallow end of the pool while a discreet trickle of water wets a rock face
and adds interest to a pergola facing the house from the far end.

The land undulates to the north of the house, which is at the apex of a
constructed hill. Grand processional steps lead down from the terrace through
jasmine planted as a ground cover to control the erosion and create a textural
contrast with the lawn. A large pond occupies the middle-distance, graced by
a shapely live oak growing on a small island. Beyond, the land sweeps up to a
sturdy rustic stone pergola, sited to catch the view of the house backed by
the rounded forms of the Santa Cruz Mountains. Nearby, a spectacular rocky
waterfall made with large rough-hewn boulders recalls Halprin's iconic water
features that still adorn public spaces across the country.

The house, walls, terrace, and steps are all limestone.

BERGSTROM PALM GARDEN
ATHERTON

When Edith Bergstrom was a young art student, home from college and wandering around with her camera looking for subjects to paint, she noticed the hatched pattern on the trunk of a palm tree. The pattern was completely abstract, but it was also realistic. The dichotomy intrigued her, and her lifelong fascination with palms was born. Palms became both her career—she is a well-known painter of palms—and her avocation. Her two-acre garden has four hundred of them and includes more than one hundred fifty different species.

After acquiring a house on a flat lot in the late 1980s, Bergstrom began to garden on a scale worthy of one born in the extensive farmlands of the Imperial Valley. She kept many of the plants from an existing Japanese garden, including cherries, magnolias, and Japanese maples, but she set about sculpting the land into a fitting home for her palms. The first big move was to rip out a pyracantha hedge and make a huge dirt berm to block the street and ensure a sense of containment. Then Bergstrom and her husband bought the neighbor's lot and demolished the house. When the contractor told her that he had trouble finding a place to put the dirt from various excavation sites, Bergstrom replied, "Bring it here!"

For several years, truckloads of dirt would arrive at this exclusive neighborhood, and Bergstrom, after having the tractor mix the dirt with yards of compost, would supervise the creation of contours in the garden. Eventually she created a landscape where the difference in elevation between the low point, at one end of a former swimming pool, and the high point, a mound now called Aussie Hill, was almost twenty feet. She also knew that she needed rocks, large rocks, to give the garden a feeling of age and permanence. After a long search, she found a crew who brought over a crane and a flatbed of rocks and, starting at the back of the lot, they lifted and placed the rocks amid the earth contours she had fashioned.

While she was sculpting the land, she was also acquiring palms. All but three of the large trees in the garden were bought as small plants, and some were

Above: Australian palms in the area Bergstrom calls Aussie Hill.

Opposite: This large multistem palm is a cross between a Canary Island date palm (*Phoenix canariensis*) and a Senegalese date palm (*Phoenix reclinata*).

grown from seed. She searched the internet for obscure varieties, went on field trips with friends from the Palm Society to specialty nurseries, and built an impressive collection of palms that do well in the Northern California climate.

Twenty years later, the garden is nearing maturity. It is a dense world unto itself, fascinating for the lay visitor, compelling for the expert. The palms are integrated into a landscape with a wider Mediterranean palette that includes succulents but also grasses, a silk floss tree, perennials, and roses. Because she's a painter and has paid great attention to the way plants look together, the eye moves easily through the garden. Individual specimens are shown to best advantage, and the garden does what it was built to do: showcase the infinite complexity and beauty of Edith Bergstrom's beloved palms.

Two king palms (*Archonto-phoenix alexandrae*) grow against the corner of the conservatory. Across the path, the cluster of small trunks topped with yellow and green fronds is the Paurotis palm (*Acoelorrhaphe wrightii*).

KAREN AND NED GILHULY GARDEN

WOODSIDE

Creating a garden from scratch can be a daunting prospect, but it helps to have a picture in your mind and a good guide. For Karen Gilhuly, the image was her grandmother's garden, where she remembered wandering as a child through different garden rooms to discover special places, whether a mossy bench or a huge orange tree. The guide was landscape architect Ron Lutsko, who was hired in 1993, right after the Gilhulys bought the property. At that time the house was under construction, and there was no landscape plan. Lutsko worked on the property for almost five years, carving out garden spaces and planting the gardens with a mixture of California natives and Mediterranean plants.

Just as the garden began to feel settled, the couple moved to London for six years. They returned every summer and could see that the plants were maturing, both for good and bad. When they moved back in 2004, they acquired some neighboring land, and the editing began in earnest. The additional acreage enabled them to expand the gardens along the true contours and topography of the property, providing some necessary breathing room. Gilhuly also wanted to infuse the planting with a new sensibility she developed by looking at great European gardens. With the help of landscape architect Peter Rosekrans, she added new gardens around the pool area and a hillside "wild garden" that includes a mini-vineyard of Pinot Noir grapes.

The lush front borders are the first indication that there is a serious gardener at work here. The sixteen-foot-deep, two-tiered beds are filled with a mix of westringia, salvia, blueberry bushes, santolina, euphorbia, and teuchrium, punctuated with red-leafed loropetalum and backed by a hedge of fragrant rhododendrons, including *Forsterianum*, *McNabii*, and *taronense*. The borders along the back of the property, which required soil amending over several years, are where Gilhuly and her "teammate," gardener Carole Kraft, can be more experimental. Those beds have become Gilhuly's most active palette— planting artichokes with agapanthus one year or trying them with lime-green

Above and opposite: The garden in front of the house is intensively planted, with mock orange (*Philadelphus* 'Belle Etoile') echoing the Eddie's White Wonder dogwood and the silvery plants in front, which include Spanish lavender (*Lavandula stoechas*) and dwarf coastal rosemary (*Westringia fruticosa* 'Grey Box').

Overleaf: Dianella surrounds this handsome trough from the south of France. Swan Hill fruitless olives line the gravel motor court. Behind the faux-bois bench is a Japanese snowbell (*Styrax japonica*), just beginning to leaf out.

Above: Two-tiered beds are filled with a complex planting.

Opposite above: Sycamores shade the back lawn. Cotinus, teucrium, Iceberg roses, and pittosporum 'Golf Ball' are planted in a rhythmic pattern in the west border.

Opposite below: Further away from the house, plant varieties are repeated but allowed to spread more loosely. Itoh peonies 'Yellow Heaven' are in the foreground.

pittosporum 'Golf Ball' another—and the place where she can keep an eye on interesting new introductions, keeping her garden looking fresh and original.

Plants are repeated throughout the property but used in different ways. Gardens further from the house are planted more informally. For instance, the euphorbia that is kept under control in the motor court is allowed to seed itself freely in the vineyard garden. Plants are moved around as well. "I like to reinvigorate spaces in my house by moving furniture, and I seem to do the same thing in my yard—with some abandon," Gilhuly points out. The result is a series of superb, mature gardens that are spread throughout the four acres, accented with handsome pieces of architectural salvage that the Gilhulys brought back from their sojourn in England.

A shaded side path leads to the rose garden and, beyond, to the back yard. Arches are covered in *Rosa* 'Cecile Brunner' and the water feature is a re-purposed part from an old olive press.

CHEROKEE FARMS

PORTOLA VALLEY

The Hunters have always had a vegetable garden, just not always a beautiful one. For years the vegetable beds were tucked away out of sight on their two-acre property, and the focus in the backyard was the large lawn dedicated to children and sports. When the youngest child went off to college, Lori Hunter had an epiphany. "We are going to put a farm back there," she announced to her husband, Deke. That was four years ago, and now they have an edible garden that is as productive as it is beautiful.

Deke Hunter had very high standards. His mother was an accomplished gardener, and he had grown up in a house with a midcentury modern garden designed by the legendary Bay Area landscape architect Thomas Church. So when they started to plan this farm, he brought back the landscape architect who had designed the garden when they acquired the house. The edible garden that Janell Denler Hobart designed sits directly behind and below the house on about three-quarters of an acre, and it is now the main event in the landscape. The "farm" makes a satisfying pattern when viewed from the house above. There are twelve raised beds, six on either side of a central fountain that is nestled in a bed of squash and sorrel. In addition, twelve fruit trees, including several varieties of antique apples, quince, peach, and cherries, spring from individual beds. A sunken, walled seating area is set into the garden on the house side, backed by espaliered Fuji and Pink Lady apples and flanked by two borders of artichokes. Completing the pattern is a long grape arbor shading a harvest table.

The Hunters have taken great care with the details and objects in the garden. Fresh-sown seeds are covered with woven cloches imported from England; the fruit tree beds are protected with wattle fencing; the harvest table built of recycled scaffolding is held up by chicken baskets from Bali; and the lighting fixtures on the pergola are made from chicken feeders. A willow tunnel started from whips tied to rebar has grown together and acts as a support for raspberries and blackberries.

Above: Cloches imported from England protect herb seedlings planted on either side of the path to the guest cottage.

Opposite: This large fig produces enough fruit for more than one hundred jars of chutney and jam.

Above: Several varieties of apple trees, underplanted with geranium 'Rozanne,' grow in wattle-enclosed beds.

The dynamic in the Hunter household is that she tends the chickens, the vegetables, the compost, and the soil, and he focuses on the aesthetics while also making sure that the garden contributes to the health and well-being of his honeybees. But if you were going to use just one word to describe this garden, it would be "abundance." Lori Hunter took the local master gardener class, and with the memory of her Italian grandparents and the help of an Italian neighbor she has turned the garden into a place of plenty. In the past, neighbors and friends were the lucky recipients of her vegetables. She loves that the garden is "interactive" and the vegetables draw people to it. But she has started to focus on organizing her production so that she can share it with others who need fresh-grown food, and she is looking forward to making her edible garden as useful as it is beautiful.

Above and below: Flowering onions and leeks growing among the lettuces provide food for beneficial insects. Cabbages at the corners of the raised beds distract slugs from the three kinds of beets, oregano, marjoram, and thyme planted here.

Overleaf: View over the garden to Windy Hill, which is part of the Peninsula Open Space Trust. Blueberries and quince grow alongside the long arbor, which supports table grapes as well as Hunter's favorite 'Polka' roses.

pounds of olives and make sixty-five gallons of olive oil. The organic vegetable garden and the flock of chickens more than feed the family, and the small working farm has become a vital area of the property.

Throughout the project, the owners were committed first and foremost to the land and were determined to "do it right," though that can often be so much more demanding than to just "get it done." It took a team effort from Trainor's office that included co-designers and project managers David LeRoy and Eefje Theeuws to create the more intense colorful landscape near the house, transition to the still-verdant bunch grasses, and feather out into the dry grassy landscape beyond. Now, although the fence of recycled grape posts marks out the property line, truly it seems more that the fence is part of the larger landscape, along with the carefully planted meadows and the distant hills, which carry the eye far beyond to a sliver of ocean on the horizon.

Above: The swimming pool sits in a raised meadow fringed with olive trees.

Overleaf: A Chinese Pistache tree stands in a field of grasses and yarrow.

BIG SWING

LA HONDA

This sprawling garden on a windswept hillside in the Santa Cruz Mountains is called Jardin de Viento, and it has been nurtured for more than thirty years by the renowned gardener and salvia expert Betsy Clebsch. The larger property itself is called Big Swing, for the adult-size swing that used to hang from a huge Douglas Fir on the lower pasture land. The house and garden face westward toward Mindego, which is Clebsch's special touchstone; the thrill for the visitor is experiencing a garden that responds specifically to its site and magnificent views while integrating the display of salvias in so many different colors and forms.

The house was built in 1984 and, soon after moving in, Clebsch planted her first garden, with crisscross

Above: Arbutus 'Marina' underlines the distant view in front of the house, accented by the pink spikes of a Puya species and the native *Salvia mellifera*.

Opposite: Clebsch's favorite view, toward Mindego and the mountains beyond, with a planting of *Echium gentianoides* in the foreground.

paths and a clever double fencing system of two rows of four-foot-tall fencing set five feet apart that keeps out the plentiful wildlife—especially the deer. Clebsch, who comes from a long line of gardeners, is originally from Virginia and still has the drawl to prove it. Her garden, reflecting the different strands of her life, is planted with a mix of sun-loving Mediterranean plants, including rosemary and lavender, classic Virginia garden stalwarts like boxwood, foxgloves, and roses, along with a mix of California natives like ceanothus and arctostaphylos. And, of course, there are salvias, which she has been experimenting with for decades. In the main garden, the salvias are planted in and among other perennials and shrubs in pleasing combinations that showcase their usefulness.

Alongside her main garden is what Clebsch calls her annex, or study garden. It is where she "kept hundreds of salvias penned up" while she was working on her first book, *A Book of Salvias*, published in 1997 (revised in 2003), and where there are still many unusual varieties. Although she has grown here only a fraction of the nine hundred species that have been identified, there is still a tremendous range. Following the 91-year-old Clebsch around the garden as she dispenses wisdom and sharply rattles off plant names is an opportunity to soak in some of her encyclopedic knowledge of the salvia family. Many of them have special stories attached, like *Salvia spathacea* 'Kawatre,' which the nurseryman Nevin

Above: Self-seeding *Geranium palmatum.*

Opposite: Pale pink blooms of *Dudleya* 'Frank Reinelt' complement the darker-hued *Salvia spathacea* 'Kawatre' in the foreground.

Smith discovered on a hiking trip in the Santa Lucia Mountains near Big Sur. There are the silvery, wooly foliage of *Salvia argentea* and the true blue color of *Salvia sinaloensis*, the California native *Salvia leucophylla* and the Chinese native *Salvia flava*, all carefully labeled for observation. The salvias, some that bloom once and some with blooming periods throughout the year, are particularly happy in this naturally temperate location, where there is sharp drainage, plentiful sun, and good airflow.

Sweeps of California natives, which require little water and thrive on the exposed, windy site, are planted along the path in front of the house. Clebsch learned to love native plants under the tutelage of Gerda Isenberg, the founder of the legendary Yerba Buena Nursery and a native plant expert. At the time, Isenberg's nursery was just down the road from Clebsch's property, and it included a two-acre demonstration garden where mature plants could be observed. Clebsch's plantings, now quite mature themselves, have blended into the natural landscape. In fact, there is a sense throughout the gardens that the larger natural world has benefited from this gardener's hand, and the proof is in the many pollinators—bees, hummingbirds, bats, moths, and flies—that are drawn to this flower-filled hillside.

Above: The deer fence is almost obscured by the *Cistus landanifer* with *Omphalodes linifolia* in front and *Centranthus ruber* and *Calendula officinalis* to the right.

Opposite: *Rosa* 'La Marne' and *Linaria purpurea* on either side of the path.

Above: *Ceanothus thyrsiflorus* var. *griesus* 'Yankee Point' is used in the garden to great effect.

Opposite: Two roses are intertwined on the rustic arbor: peach-colored 'Juane Desprez' and pink 'Frances E Lester.' In the foreground is *Salvia blepharophylla*.

LAGUNA RANCH

SANTA CRUZ

Before Stephanie and David Mills bought this property in 1991, it had already had several failed incarnations. It was cleared for oil and gas exploration that never materialized, although asphaltum was discovered and there's still a small quarry on the property today. There was an unsuccessful attempt to grow Brussels sprouts as a commercial crop, but at least the ground had been broken and plowed. Finally, it was used to graze cattle, who didn't mind the thistles, poison oak, and non-native grasses. There was no house and no one had ever tried to garden here, but Stephanie Mills, who is originally English and "born gardening," began to plant as soon as the first buildings started to go up.

Above: Meadow planting of Libertia.

Opposite: The fan shapes of the aloe, agave, bryophyllum, and eucomis resonate with the canopy of the acacia trees above.

Grass expert John Greenlee helped establish the first gardens, which were almost exclusively ornamental grasses that served as good placeholders for the gardens that were to come. Over time, Mills, who claims to have known nothing about the soil, weather, and climate when she moved to this hillside, gradually became an expert in the ecology of her 390 acres. The wind was fierce, and there was just one native willow for windbreak so one of her first projects was to plant trees: "The wind blew so hard up here that it blew my dog off the deck outside the house," she recalls. Although the grasses that Greenlee installed flourished and competed strongly with the existing invasives, Mills became interested in finding other plants that would have more diversity in color, texture, and form.

In 2001 Mills started to seriously develop other gardens, and she asked David Leroy, a garden designer from Santa Cruz, to help make the plans in her head a reality. Like Mills, who is fearless in trying plants out, Leroy was willing to take risks and experiment with plant material. Her mantra was "Buy what you like—if it dies twice, ditch it." Together they established a series of gardens that are spread over ten acres around the house, including a sunrise and sunset garden, a moon garden, an orchard and vegetable garden, a children's garden, a teepee garden, and several pond gardens.

This hillside that had seemed so inhospitable at first has turned out to be an ideal place to garden as long as everything is planted in gopher baskets. It's a place where "anything you put in the ground grows—not just grows, but flowers, flourishes, takes care of itself, and multiplies." There is an extensive trail network throughout the larger property, and Mills has worked with the local Amah Mutsun tribe to explore archaeological sites along Laguna Creek. As she says, "We're here and the land was here before us and will be after us and it's completely vulnerable to what we do to it. If one can be a good steward, why not?"

Above: Plum trees stand in front of a border of Watsonia and iris.

Opposite: Olives, with aloe, euphorbia, and mint in bloom.

Overleaf: Chartreuse euphorbia naturalized in front of the "Armory" next to the house.

Above: Mounded euphorbia
contrasts with the upright restios, with crocosmia providing
a pop of color.

Opposite: A path leads through
Stipa gigantea to the wilder
part of the property.

Above: An informal planting of melaleuca, plectranthus, and agapanthus on the hillside below the house.

Opposite: A pair of Adirondack chairs face west to the Pacific Ocean.

SAN FRANCISCO

A CITY GARDEN
PACIFIC HEIGHTS

The centerpiece of this property is the handsome 1932 stucco house designed by Albert Farr, which is surrounded by a series of garden rooms that match its proportions. The hardscape was designed by landscape architect Ron Herman in 1997, shortly after the owners moved in, transforming the rather pedestrian backyard into a rich and varied space. Seventeen trees were planted, including several fruit trees and a grove of Japanese maples, and twelve garden zones with varying cultural requirements were established.

The planting areas flow from one to the other, with a maple walk as the tranquil connector between the formality of the front terrace and the more relaxed back garden. A multi-trunked purple beech towering over the roof of the house is a graceful and venerable presence. The landscape designer Beryt Oliver has created an elaborate planting that reflects the interplay between the textures and colors of house and garden. The long potager border is a mix of flowers for cutting and fruit and vegetables for harvesting. Herbs, artichokes, blueberries, strawberries, and asparagus grow among the roses, poppies, foxgloves, peonies, delphiniums, allium, and milkweed. Already an attractive garden for pollinators like bees, hummingbirds, and butterflies, the owners continue to fine-tune the plantings to attract even more.

Above: A Sally Holmes rose climbs on top of the pergola, with *Hebe* 'Wistley Blue' at the base of the columns.

Opposite: Purple beech is underplanted with oak leaf hydrangea (*Hydrangea quercifolia* 'Alice'), which remains evergreen in the winter.

A series of small front garden rooms faces the street. The succulent panel hanging on the far wall is filled with thyme, arabis, heuchera, leptinella, graptoveria, and echeveria.

Above: In the shady maple walk on the side of the house, tree ferns and Japanese maples stand in a woodland planting of mini plants that are all white-flowering, including bleeding heart (*Dicentra spect-abilis* 'Alba') that blooms in the early spring.

Opposite: A side border is filled with a mix of flowers and herbs that attract pollinators, including foxgloves, garden chives, and two eye-catching pink 'Keiko' Itoh peonies.

JANE MCLAUGHLIN GARDEN

PACIFIC HEIGHTS

Fifteen years ago, Jane McLaughlin asked designer Elizabeth Everdell to re-do her backyard so she could finally garden, as her mother had before her. No matter that it was tiny and the existing plant material consisted of only a tree fern, a lemon tree, and a Cecile Brunner rose creeping over the garden room about three-quarters of the way to the back boundary. Everdell obliged with a garden whose clear, simple lines are satisfying when seen from the main living rooms on the second floor, but allows real scope for a keen gardener in the two long flower beds that flank a central tapis vert. Everdell installed anchor plants and gave McLaughlin some excellent advice: choose a color palette and stay with it.

And she has. It is still all pink to blue to white, but the rest is now McLaughlin's show and she loves it. Every morning she brings her coffee out to the garden to enjoy, but also to observe, and in this way, she has taught herself to garden. She has fallen in love with roses, which she has inserted everywhere in her flowerbeds, but also in a small cutting garden she maintains on the far side of the garden house. There, sixty roses flourish, and if for some reason she loses one, like the experienced gardener she has become, she relishes the opportunity of finding an even better specimen to take its place.

Above and opposite: The right side of the garden is very shady, and the left sunny, but careful planting ensures that both beds are equally bright and colorful.

McLaughlin supplements the permanent planting with a colorful display of flowers in containers that change with the seasons.

RENA BRANSTEN GARDEN
PRESIDIO HEIGHTS

When Rena Bransten found her Mediterranean-style house forty-five years ago, one of its most appealing features was an unusually large and flat backyard. For a woman with small children, an enclosed back garden that opened directly from floor-to-ceiling windows in the living room was a great find, and it has been a continuing source of pleasure since then. Bransten had not yet started her eponymous art gallery, but she was clearly a visual person. Since the garden is the backdrop to her living area, she was passionately interested in how it would look. Aerin Moore of Magic Gardens Landscaping was able to translate her aesthetic into a space that is both bold and cozy, suitable for someone deeply involved in contemporary art, and beautiful enough to be the largest "painting" in the house.

Bransten wanted variation, texture, and, if there was color, it had to be strong—no pastel flowers here. Moore's practice of assembling a plant palette and then putting the plants together on site worked perfectly. The mix is entirely visual and not about a particular genre of garden. There are plenty of succulents and many subtropicals as well as some boxwood and roses, nine different fuchsias and many abutilon. It all works together as a setting for *The Three Graces*, Bransten's name for the larger-than-life ceramic figures by the artist Viola Frey, which are the central focus of the garden.

Above: Viola Frey's *The Three Graces* are framed in a living room window.

Opposite: Organic forms and bold colors characterize the planting, seen in the red and purple fuchsias and the strappy golden foliage of the cordyline.

Above and opposite: The stone path provides structure to the dense planting, which is conceived more as an abstract painting than a traditional garden. The textures and tints of pittosporum, dwarf mugo pine, loropetalum, *Libertia peregrinans*, aeonium 'Cyclops,' and phormium 'Yellow Wave' create a rich tapestry.

NASH GARDEN

THE CASTRO

This garden on the top of a windy hill is actually a fully functioning driveway that is used on a daily basis. The transformation from driveway to garden was a collaborative effort between designer Dan Carlson of Wiggglestem Gardens and his client, Madeleine Nash, who researched different varieties of succulents and thyme and helped to set the overall aesthetic tone of the garden. The mosaic pattern of the permeable driveway filled with creeping mint plays off the center strip of thyme, sempervivum, and echeveria.

"I wanted to get low, to have the whole show right on the ground," says Carlson. Although the plant palette is limited, there is plenty of seasonal interest, with an intense carpet of rich purple color in spring that fades in summer to a purplish brown. Fall and winter show off the intricate tapestry of green and gray. Carlson used several different thymes, including slow-growing wooly thyme, lime thyme, and creeping thyme, and intermingled miniature gray-purple sedum to achieve his effect. The accent plantings along each side are strips of silver *Dymondia margaretae*, a South African drought-tolerant ground cover. Although sometimes a few inflorescent spikes of the echeveria get nipped by a car pulling in, overall, nothing is taller than six inches and the garden is surprisingly resilient.

Above and opposite: The checkerboard pattern on the garage door plays off the shape of the creeping mint-filled pavers. Next to the front door is bougainvillea under-planted with *Senecio vitalis* 'Serpents' and aeonium in bloom.

Overleaf: Different varieties of creeping thyme form a dense mat, highlighted with sempervivums, *Echeveria derosa* (left) and *Echeveria elegans* (center).

LENORE PEREIRA AND RICH NILES GARDEN

SOUTH PARK

Lenore Pereira and Rich Niles moved to this contemporary house overlooking a small, historic public park from Berkeley, where they had a large garden designed by the artist and garden designer Harlan Hand, a master at working with color and unusual plants, especially succulents. This tiny garden on an upper deck of the house, designed by the landscape architect Loretta Gargan, is an homage to Hand's earlier work: a softly carpeted garden room with a great variety of succulents and grasses set against the angular urban landscape of downtown. The garden also provides a perfect miniaturized world for Kiki Smith's sculpture *Three Harpies*.

The concrete stepping stones, designed by the architects of the house, Luke Ogrydziak and Zoe Prillinger, seem to be set in a random pattern, but they have been arranged to create little twists and turns through the space so that there are always different views, never a linear experience. Every inch of the garden seems valued and considered. The current gardener, King Sip, who was the longtime head gardener at Strybing Arboretum in Golden Gate Park, brings an artist's eye to her meticulous plantings, which have now grown together to form a dense mat of intricate, vegetal pattern with a pleasing mix of color, texture, and form.

Above and oppposite: A mixed planting of succulents and grasses softens the rectilinear lines of the house, pathway, skylights, and cityscape.

Overleaf: Textured miniatures weave together and overflow the paths among the concrete pavers creating the setting for Kiki Smith's *Three Harpies*.

URBAN SPRING

GLEN PARK

Jenn and Marcel Wilson's garden hits the sweet spot between edgy design and the warm, comforting feeling of a family garden connected to nature. Its graphic lines and modern shapes can be enjoyed from the top two decks, and it includes sophisticated plant combinations and a lawn for kids to play on. Back in the early 2000s, when the Wilsons came upon the partially renovated house, it had an almost unusable sloping backyard. What sold them on the property was the natural stream bubbling up at the foot of the back steps. As landscape architects, they knew that the stream was a gift, not a problem.

While the house renovation was being completed, the Wilsons designed and built the 20-by-50-foot garden. The dirt from excavating the basement was used to make a flat lawn. Discarded steel beams from the house were cut up and used as supports for the decks and the stairs. Where the water bubbled up, they built a three-sided catch basin so they could see the water, then put together a series of copper runnels as a channel down to the end of the garden so they could hear it, and made a water garden featuring Louisiana Iris at the end of the garden so they could appreciate what water can do.

Above: Louisiana, Siberian, and Japanese variegated iris grow in a water garden, screening the seating at the bottom of the garden. The back wall is covered with clematis.

Opposite: All the red steel beams used for the balcony and stair supports are recycled from the house renovation. The copper water channel is just visible through the foliage. In front of the deck is a vine maple (*Acer circinatum*).

A moss collection is displayed on the porch in front of a bed of Giant Chain fern (*Woodwardia fimbriata*).

URBAN PLAYSCAPE
MISSION DISTRICT

The brief was a little discouraging for a garden designer: a no-maintenance garden with a water feature but no plants, synthetic grass where children could play safely, and a total area of 1,800 square feet. The results are anything but discouraging: an engaging, water-themed garden where traditional and contemporary building techniques complement each other, where there is lots of creative play space, several vibrant living walls, a large water wall that has great visual impact but takes up very little square footage, and every inch now usable and decorative outdoor space.

In this case, it helps that the designer, Monica Viarengo, is Italian. The Genovese craftsmen she brought in to do the paving took over four weeks to execute the clean modern design inspired by concentric waves of water. The narrow side yard, usually the most dismal part of a small lot, is a tour de force, where the patterns of the paving, begun in the tiny front yard, provide a visual link to the larger space in the back. Although the owners originally thought they weren't garden people at all, they have come to appreciate the varied plantings of ferns, heuchera, oxalis, lysimachia, and campanula, among others, that now decorate their walls. Best of all, the sophisticated space has become lively and totally family friendly.

Above: Artisans from Genoa were brought in to execute this water-inspired pebble design.

Opposite: The side yard is clean, bright, and eminently usable. A large water wall animates the garden without taking up too much space.

The living walls are the real garden, here decorating the children's slide. The artificial turf is a durable year-round play surface.

DIAMOND STREET GARDEN
THE CASTRO

So often in the hills of San Francisco the backyard either goes up or down. In the case of this garden, the house sits right on the sidewalk and a sliver of a backyard goes straight up four stories—so steeply that when the owners bought the house they had no safe way of accessing the top of the lot with its outstanding view of the city, and the yard was in danger of sliding down into the house. Faced with difficult technical issues and a strong desire for flowers and a cutting garden, they selected Surfacedesign, a landscape architecture firm that they felt could handle both the site and the horticultural challenges.

For a firm that does some of the most cutting-edge work around, Surfacedesign is surprisingly plant and flower friendly. The designers are particularly adept at engaging with the client and the land in a three-way dialogue that can have original results. The giant bowl-shaped retaining wall painted plum, which was the owner's choice, is a bold, clean, and unusual shape and a delightful foil for burgeoning plant life. Installing a cutting garden on this steep and windy slope was a problem, but Richard Darrough, expert horticulturalist, has planted a matrix of appropriately tough and pleasing specimens. The elegantly detailed stair curving around the wall and across the garden adds coherence and structure to the space and leads to the viewing deck at the top of the garden.

Above and opposite: The bowl-shaped retaining wall is a pleasing and playful way to deal with the steep slope. Allium and Japanese anemones nestle in the steps.

Teucrium fruticans and leonotis mingle with salvias, allium, melianthus, alternanthera, and stachys in the beds flanking the path. *Euphorbia rigens* and beschorneria grow by the hot tub.

Above and opposite: Concrete pavers are embedded vertically in the steps; at the bottom, baby's tears (*soleirolia soleirolii*) grows between them.

CLIFF HOUSE

TELEGRAPH HILL

When they bought the 1920s house that appears to cling to a cliff overlooking the waterfront, the owners turned to landscape architect Andrea Cochran to reconfigure the entrance. Her surprising sculptural design creates a memorable sequence of ramps and steps leading to the main living quarters. At different levels, two Corten steel balconies jut out abruptly over the cliff, and they appear to lack any barrier to the abyss below. A closer look reveals a glass wall, and the stunning view pulls braver visitors out to the edge.

Although the details are precise and sophisticated, the materials—Corten steel, concrete, and wood—are rougher, in keeping with the rugged shale and sandstone cliff below. The industrial quality of the Corten steel seems a direct reference to the old warehouse buildings far below. In contrast to the drama of the entranceway, a shade garden behind the house radiates serenity and calm, reminiscent of a meditation garden. It is primarily a viewing garden, visible right through the ground floor of the house, but the rounded rocks in the gravel courtyard are heated and a pleasant resting spot on a cool San Francisco day.

Above and opposite: The strong shapes and contemporary materials of Andrea Cochran's design complement the bold architecture.

Above and opposite: Eucalyptus
emerging from the fog makes
a natural scrim over the cityscape. The contrast with the

concrete and Corten steel is
particularly effective.

Above and opposite: The shady Zen garden is at the back of the house, but it is visible from many places on the ground floor. Artificial "rocks" can be warmed to make it a pleasant place on cool days.

EAST BAY

JON KAPLAN AND
JULIE BILLINGS GARDEN
PIEDMONT

This elegant house designed by Willis Polk was much bigger than anything that Jon Kaplan and Julie Billings had been considering buying, but they were attracted to its graceful lines and its 105-year-old, 1.5-acre garden. The house and garden predate Polk's masterpiece, Filoli. Here, unlike at Filoli, Polk designed the garden as well, and the house and garden present a seamless unit.

Polk's client was businessman and philanthropist James Kennedy Moffitt, for whom Moffitt Library at the University of California at Berkeley is named. Moffitt, who died in 1955, was an avid book lover and gardener. A memorial article in the California Historical Society archives reports: "In his library and garden in Piedmont, he found refreshment from a busy workweek schedule. His tastes and interests led him to assemble one of the largest and most important collections of incunabula in the west, and a beautiful garden always bore evidence of his own care and skill."

Above: Wisteria runs along the front of the house.

Opposite: The red-brick herringbone paving and many of the trees are original to the garden. Kaplan and Billings encourage a full planting in the beds, which are edged with teucrium. Senecio has self-sown throughout, and the bold shapes of the red phormium lead the eye down to the lower terrace.

That beautiful garden was in decline by the time that Kaplan and Billings bought the property in 2012, but Polk's herringbone-patterned brick terraces were still there and Moffitt's magnificent trees had reached maturity. The first order of business was to get the irrigation system working and to lay in a watering system for the rest of the garden; this Kaplan did himself with the help of a gardener, digging the trenches and laying the pipes.

Once Kaplan and Billings had reversed the decline, they were free to indulge their passion for plants. They have respectfully preserved the structure of the garden, the formal terraces and hedging, the rose garden, and the parterres, but within these boundaries there is an increasingly diverse plant community. Taking their cues from what was already there, they have augmented as well as added. When they bought the property, there were a number of large, sickly-looking tree ferns. Once the irrigation was repaired, they began to look better so dozens more have been added, animating the understory of the shady part of the garden. Kaplan is fond of brugmansias, and there are now twenty

Above: The parterre is composed of teucrium and boxwood, with the sword-like leaves of phormium in the center. The urns in the foreground with the red phormium are original to the property.

Opposite: Teucrium, golden oregano, and lavender mingle in the beds beside the path. A rich mix of leaf color, including red berberis and loropetalum, ensures that the vibrant mood continues as the garden flows down the hill from the house.

different varieties. Kaplan and Billings have different gardening styles and skills: Kaplan likes controlled chaos, Billings likes neat—a good combination when dealing with this complexity, because if it were too chaotic the classic structure would disappear, if too tidy the heart would go out of the garden. As it is, it has once more become "a beautiful garden" bearing evidence of a new generation's "care and skill."

Once the original tree ferns were brought back to health, Kaplan and Billings added many more.

MARCIA DONAHUE GARDEN
BERKELEY

It is hard to overestimate the influence that Marcia Donahue's small (60-by-100-foot) garden has had on gardens up and down San Francisco Bay. Her sculptures and adventurous attitude toward plants turns up in gardens from Santa Cruz to Napa. Donahue was an art school graduate focused on textiles when she moved to this two-story Victorian house almost forty years ago. Even as she was renovating the dilapidated house, she plunged into what has been her life's work—creating gardens and art. In one of the many interviews she has given over the years, she said of her garden, "It is not intended to be a tasteful setting for the house; it is a setting for personal expression and experience." And she has shared this personal expression with a constant stream of visitors who are welcomed to the garden every Sunday afternoon. Her philosophy, along with her stunningly diverse plant palette and her weirdly compelling sculpture, has given countless gardeners from the Bay Area and further afield permission to walk a little way on the wild side as they create their own gardens.

The garden has long since reached maximum capacity with plants from every continent jostling for position: from New Zealand's Shaving Brush Palm, the South African restio, and the Australian grass tree to old-fashioned roses. Early on she planted the sides of her garden so thickly that the foliage often meets overhead, deliberately creating a sense of enclosure to enhance the feeling of a world apart. Curved paths lead to several destinations, including the raised koi pond filled with waterlilies and the "poultry pagoda," where twenty bantam chickens live happily amid the jungle of plants.

Above: Sprites and colorful leaf-shapes atop bamboo-like stems are interspersed with the plants.

Opposite: The "poultry pagoda" is made from items recycled from the dump, including old bedsprings and glass lampshades on the roof. Bantams peck at the fallen flowers of the red mallow (*Malvaviscus arboreus*).

The raised koi pond is surrounded by lush planting
and found objects. The
blue spheres are old fishing
floats and the two logs with
bracket fungi are examples of
Donahue's ceramics.

VERA AND JOHN PARDEE GARDEN

BERKELEY

The first time John and Vera Pardee saw their romantic 1930s-era Spanish Revival villa it "captured our hearts." The Pardees were not plant experts or even gardeners. What they did not fully realize when they bought their home in 2010 was that they were also taking on a remarkable garden with an impressive pedigree. It was designed by Brandon Tyson in collaboration with the previous owner. Tyson, one of the leading garden makers of the Bay Area, creates theatrical, plant-centric gardens that start with a strong structure and overlay this with exotic and often extraordinary plant specimens, gardens full of controlled chaos and high drama: gardens that need attention.

The first challenge for the Pardees was finding someone to pay that attention. The extensive and unusual plant palette of rare specimens closely planted required a high level of skill and knowledge to maintain. The task was far beyond the scope of the professionals they brought in. "This is fantastic" was the common reaction, "but you must find someone more skilled to look after it." So the Pardees ended up learning what they could from each consultant and taking on the task of guiding this garden to maturity themselves. It has been fun, and now names like *Brunsvigia josephinae* and *Jubaea chilensis* roll off the tongue.

The garden occupies the sloping space between the street and the house and is organized around a central allée that leads to a brightly tiled fountain. The colorful tiles were specially made, inspired by a fountain designed in the 1920s by Arthur and Nina Zwebell for the historic Andalusia apartment complex in Los Angeles. Part of the inspiration behind the garden is an evocation of an underwater kingdom, which explains the choice of plants with decidedly unusual shapes and sizes. Instead of a classically shaped tree form, tree aloes (*Aloe barbarae*) with sturdy, stubby trunks and unruly fronds line the allée. The fountain is shaded by three magnificent Himalayan fishtail palms (*Cayota gigas*), and erupting from the gravel all over the garden are a myriad

Above: Mangave 'Macho Mocha' and Bird of Paradise (*Strelitzia*) in front of *Tibouchina semidecandra*.

Opposite: A magnificent combination of blue-gray foliage succulents includes *Chamaerops humilis*, Agave 'Sharkskin,' *Uncinia uncinata*, *Aloe striata*, and Agave 'Victoria-Regina.'

Overleaf: Marcia Donahue's mala beads are looped over the Aloe trees (*Aloe barberae*), which form the central allée, with Leucadendron 'Cloudbank Jenny' in the foreground and Arabian aloe (*Aloe rubroviolacea*) and *Aloe marlothii*.

of colorful agaves, aeonium, and echeverias. Marcia Donahue's bamboo sculptures and her bead necklaces lend their whimsy to the ensemble.

That's not to say there are only oddities. The Pardees take great pleasure when the twenty-five or so abutilon put on their brilliant show, and they enjoy the surprises the garden brings, as when one blue mist flower (*Bartlettina sordida*) ends up being twenty. But there also are problems to solve, like replacing the hedge of fragrant, yellow-flowering *Azara dentata*, which had failed to thrive, with the more drought-tolerant and dependable crossberry. The Pardees' strategy is to keep as many of their precious specimens alive as possible while still being conscientious stewards of the environment. This grows out of their approach to the garden in general: they inherited a fantasy and they are trying to keep the dream alive.

Above: Bright orange-red
blooms of *Aloe marlothii* in
front of the trunk of the giant
fishtail palm (*Caryota gigas*).
The golden foliage of the
Australian tree fern (*Cyathea
cooperi*) forms a background.

Opposite: A gravel path leads
past *Leucadendron salignum
x laureolum* 'Rising Sun' and
Leucadendron gandogeri
into a thicket of giant timber
bamboo (*Bambusa oldhamii*)
and bell reed (*Cannomois*

virgata). There is a dark-red
aeonium (*Aeonium arboreum*
'Schwartzkopf') on the left.

RANCHO DIABLO

LAFAYETTE

A week after the owners bought this twenty-acre property with its panoramic view of Mount Diablo, the Loma Prieta earthquake struck and part of the house collapsed. The couple soon repaired the house and then planted a garden that reminded them of the Southwestern landscape that they admired—mostly cactus, but also some palms and succulents. In 1991, the winter after planting the garden, a one-hundred-year-freeze killed more than half the plants. Instead of giving up, or throwing out the planting plan, they took this as "a great education in high-desert, cold-tolerant cactus. Anything that made it through that winter we knew would probably make it for the rest of our lives."

Above: Banks of aloe in bloom with a view of the Las Trampas Regional Wilderness.

Opposite: A massed planting of opuntia in front of the house, with a *Washingtonia filifera* towering over the roof.

Three gardens—the Ruth Bancroft Garden, just a few miles away, the Huntington in Pasadena, and Lotusland in Santa Barbara—have inspired the owners. One owner, an architect, articulates the overall design and specifies the size and shape of the plants that he wants, and the other, a landscape designer and experienced horticulturist, goes out and finds the right plant material. It is a process that pushes her to accomplish what she sometimes thinks will be impossible, and it explains why their gardens are so visually satisfying. The cactus garden, which could easily have looked like a collector's hodgepodge, is instead made up of large groupings of a small palette of interesting plants that are repeated throughout.

Cactus was not being widely used in gardens when they started so it was difficult to find plants locally in anything larger than six-inch pots. They were fortunate to hear about a cactus-collecting doctor in Malibu whose garden was being dismantled, and they drove down and put as many large specimens as they could in a thirty-foot U-Haul. Those plants are now the mature backbone of the garden. Water is used sparingly: they never water the cactus, relying only on whatever water nature brings, and elsewhere on the property they control the irrigation manually. As the designer says, "When you see things in the desert, some specimens look great, some not, depending on the year. Sharp drainage is

the key to long-term survival—everything is always planted on a slope, even an artificial slope, so that water will drain away from the base of the plant."

After planting the cactus gardens around the house, the designers installed a vegetable garden on the lower part of the property. Soon they added a small circular lawn, which at first was used for training the dogs, and a fruitery, which now has fifty trees, including plums, apricots, figs, citrus, apples, and pears. Over time, the palm and agave border was added and the patch of lawn became an elegant garden space. Most importantly, it became the setting for the five statues from the old San Francisco Library that they had bought at auction. Now, with its entirely different mood, this part of the property has become a much-used retreat, completely encircled by lush planting beds and a dramatic aloe hedge setting off the spectacular view.

Above: Statues from the old San Francisco Library are set among *Chamaerops humilis* var. *argentea* and *Agave americana*.

Opposite: A jelly palm (*Butia capitata*), underplanted with *Chamaerops humilis* var. *argentea*.

Overleaf: Two large, gnarly *Cereus peruvianus* 'Monstrosus,' with *Cephalocereus senilis* and assorted *Trichocereus* hybrids.

FLORA GRUBB GARDEN

BERKELEY

Flora Grubb, whose emporium of the same name in southeast San Francisco is a magnet for gardeners and designers looking for bold and unusual plants, has a home garden where she practices what she preaches. It's a carefully executed tapestry of different shades of green in deftly designed beds filled with interesting plants. Grubb designed the garden to be "very even, very soft on the eyes, nothing that will grab the eye and not let go. This is a place of relaxation, resting, rejuvenating."

This is also clearly the home of someone who loves plants. Every day, she's out in the garden pinching, shaping, and pruning, and she tries out plants from the shop in different places, knowing that she can change her mind and take them back if they don't work. Several choice specimens, including Rhipsalis and Euphorbia 'Cat Tails,' are showcased in pots alongside the house under the eaves, where they benefit from the dryer conditions. Acacias are a special interest; there are many in the garden, including a large *Acacia cognata* by the house and its sport Acacia 'Cousin Itt', so soft it invites stroking, interplanted with boxwood in the main planting bed. The garden, though small and tightly planted, is always in flux—plants creep out into the negative space and have to be nipped back, plants die and get replaced, and always there are new plants to try out.

Above: Ceaonothus 'Diamond Heights' creeps along in front of Acacia 'Cousin Itt' and aeonium.

Opposite: *Brahea armata* 'Clara' shades the front garden planted with *Polypodium guttatum*, Leucadendron 'Crown Jubilee,' Cotinus 'Golden Spirit', *Cannomois grandis*, and Aeonium 'Mint Saucer.'

Above: A graceful, weeping form and a reputation for drought tolerance make Acacia 'Cousin Itt' a very useful plant in the front garden.

Opposite: *Acacia cognata* next to the house. The large-leafed plant near the front door is an unusual specimen of *Meryta sinclairii* 'Moonlight.'

VANESSA KUEMMERLE GARDEN

EMERYVILLE

Vanessa Kuemmerle's colorful front yard is part performance piece, part public service, and all garden. A vibrant kaleidoscope of shape and color, it overflows the space on the three public faces of her house. She has lived on this corner in Emeryville since 1993 and, even before she made the garden, for the ten years she was just a renter, she used her plot to enliven the neighborhood with three ten-foot, fiberglass "Doggie Diner" dog heads in her yard. When she eventually bought the house and started to plant, the corner was already a landmark.

A former art student who found her calling creating gardens, Kuemmerle seeks to produce an environment that appeals to all the senses, where the colors are vibrant, the textures appealing, and the scents divine, where you can hear the plants rustling and the birds chirping, and where there is always a little something to eat. That's why she put the Michelia alba near the sidewalk so passersby can enjoy the fragrance and fruit trees so locals can help themselves to the bounty. Slowly, she is changing the look of the neighborhood; she gardens the house next door, and helps the people across the street. Because of the configuration of her land, but even more because of the nature of her approach— "I garden in public" —her garden has become her gift to her community.

Above: The hand-carved door was acquired in Bali on a Hortisexuals tour.

Opposite: In the yard that Kuemmerle shares with her neighbors are a 'Sally Holmes' rose and a blue hesper or Mexican blue palm (*Brahea armata*).

The colors of the house blend with the garden and the blue hesper palm. Planters of the appropriately named Phormium 'Guardian' flank the front steps.

CHRIS CARMICHAEL AND TERRY STEIN GARDEN

OAKLAND

The unusual magenta blooms of the bottlebrush tree growing from the sidewalk planting strip flag this garden from blocks away. From down the street the small lot seems to be all plants, starting with a huge gold-leaved *Podocarpus totara* looming over the garden and a stately king palm at the corner. Closer inspection reveals a well-designed entrance pergola covered with wisteria 'Caroline' and a *Passiflora membranacea* vine grown for its attractive marked leaves. In the front yard alone there are seven palms in addition to the myriad other specimens, from a variegated geranium to Xanthorrhoea, growing merrily in the tiny space.

Chris Carmichael is a scientist with a PhD in zoology and a lifelong engagement with horticulture. In the garden he shares with his husband, Terry Stein, the negotiation between the scientist and the aesthete is ongoing. Carmichael particularly loves trying new plants that push the limits of what can be grown in Northern California, not surprising since he recently retired as associate director of collections and horticulture at the University of California Botanical Garden. The plant collections have changed during the twenty years Carmichael and Stein have lived here: some plants, like the *Psoralea pinnata*, have gone out of favor; some have remained staples—any plant from New Zealand; but the skill in putting the diverse specimens together in a way that brings as much joy to the visitor as to the obsessive gardener has only increased.

Above: In the backyard, several roses, including 'Betty Boop,' are growing together; next to them are windmill palm (*Trachycarpus*) and *Cordyline australis* 'Sundowner.'

Opposite: Wisteria 'Caroline' and *Passiflora membranacea* meet on the entrance pergola.

An unusual purple bottlebrush (*Callistemon*) is planted in the growing strip in front of the house; a golden totara (*Podocarpus totara* 'Aurea') towers behind it, with a Mexican blue palm (*Brahea armata*) underneath.

MARIN
SONOMA
NAPA

I'LEE HOOKER GARDEN

TIBURON

For thirty years, I'Lee Hooker's garden has been her inspiration, her hobby, and her vocation. Hooker was a ceramic artist when she moved to this three-quarter-acre hillside property in Tiburon. The garden captured Hooker's imagination, and she slowly started to work in it rather than making sculpture for it. She phased out ceramics and turned to photography, recording "the flowers, birds, and bugs" she found on the hillside. The more closely she examined her garden, the more it inspired her, and she began making exquisite scans of single flowers in their many stages of development. Later she created artist books combining her photographs and texts in unusual ways.

Above: A pale-yellow froth of kangaroo paws (*Anigozanthos*) in front of a stack of bee hives.

Opposite: Hooker created destinations, like the seating area with the two brick chairs, to encourage exploration of the whole hillside.

Topher Delaney designed the bones of the garden—the path from the house and deck down the steep hill to a flattened landing with a small lawn and a pool. Hooker then took over, creating a lush, exciting garden full of texture and immediacy, using dark-leaved, lime-colored, and variegated plants in rich and intense combinations. As she worked on the hillside, she was careful to provide destinations and reasons to explore it fully. An arbor with a swing, a bench, a set of artist's chairs are each carefully sited at focal moments in the garden. She kept the oaks, which provide needed shade and also frame the long view. At the top of the steps, she installed a tall stack of hives where resident bees produce a great deal of honey.

The sunny upper portion of the hillside is covered with a dazzling display of succulents. When questioned about this passage, Hooker points out that she was born in Palm Springs, and these are the plants of her childhood, to which she has an almost unconscious affinity. Otherwise, she has chosen plants with an eye to fullness and texture and pleasing plant associations—except of course for the roses, mostly in shades of yellow and orange. She planted them because she can't do without them, and she revels in their form and fragrance.

Above: A colorful succulent display enlivens a hot, dry section of the hillside.

Opposite: Hooker was a ceramic artist for twenty years before she turned to gardening; the three upright terra-cotta forms are hers.

Overleaf: From the terrace, the view stretches out over San Francisco Bay to the city itself.

Over the years, Hooker became a master gardener and lectured on her garden using her own photographs, inspired by the thousands of stories of life she found all around her. Now, struggling with climate extremes and the inevitable issues of aging that make running up and down her hillside more of a challenge, Hooker's relationship with the garden is more tempered. She has simplified the planting, looking for less intensity and more repose. Ironically, this has changed but not in any way diminished its impact.

COURTYARD GARDEN

At the entrance to this elegant, contemporary house the eye is caught by an exquisite harbinger of the garden to come. Like a poetic image from a Japanese print, a single Deodar cedar is outlined against a Corten steel wall. The tree leans left and its sparse horizontal branches fill the frame made by the panels of this segment of the courtyard wall, the bluish green of the needles set off by the characteristic rust color of the metal. Two large rocks are set beneath the tree, which is growing from a pillowy bed of mondo grass.

The house and courtyard were conceived as one, both profoundly influenced by a Japanese aesthetic of restraint. Every detail is resolved, every object, every view carefully considered. There were two guiding concerns in the design: the play of light throughout the day and its impact both within and without, and the views both from inside out and outside in. The firm of Aidelin Darling designed the house and courtyard, including all the hardscape in the garden, the pool, the walkways, and the courtyard walls; Ron Herman designed the initial landscape; and the owners chose and placed most of the elements with the help of Tim O'Shea of Greenworks Gardens.

Above: The scholar's stone was chosen and placed by John Nishizawa.

Opposite: European white birch was selected for its graceful form and four seasons of interest. Liriope and Berkeley sedge are planted on either side of the path.

The Japanese influence permeates the courtyard, an idealized landscape of a meadow with a creek running through it. But it is much bigger, looser, and freer than a typical Japanese courtyard garden. Here, the creek is dry, and the grasses, Berkeley sedge on one side of the creek and liriope on the other, have a lumpy, un-manicured quality that says California and not Japan. Most of the trees are deciduous, ensuring four seasons of interest. This is especially true of the Japanese maples, which change from the bright red of the new foliage, through green, to their well-known fall color before their delicate branching

A Deodar cedar stands out against the Corten steel panels of the garden wall.

Above: The vegetable beds were designed by Ron Herman and are cared for by Mika Marsui.

Opposite above: Yoshino flowering cherries (*Prunus yedoensis* 'Akebono').

Opposite below: Split-leaf Japanese maples offer delicate shapes and good fall color.

habit is fully visible in the winter. The cherries, with their fleeting bloom, are another nod to Japan, but the dominant trees in the courtyard meadow are birch, chosen for their elegance in all seasons and the graceful way their branches move through the fog and wind.

One of the successes of this garden is the artful integration of rocks into the landscape. The owners found many of them, and they had specialist John Nishizawa place them. Of particular note is the scholar's rock at the end of a long hallway within the house. Throughout, views of the garden are integral to the architecture; floor-to-ceiling windows in the front hall encourage a close-up view of the narrow "jewel garden" filled with hellebores and spring ephemerals.

Before the house and courtyard were finished, the vegetable garden, located on the coastal side of the house and also designed by Herman, was installed and functioning. The owners are invested in food production, and the specially built concrete planters are filled with vegetables grown in concert by a Japanese gardener and the owner's chef so that everything is flawlessly laid out and grown, and every morsel produced is used.

KATE AND YAZ KREHBIEL GARDEN

SAN ANSELMO

Memories of Italy spurred the design of Kate and Yaz Krehbiel's hillside garden, and indeed the finished landscape, with the mature Mediterranean cypresses in the background, does conjure up an Italian garden. The boxwood parterres and clipped balls of boxwood and Little Ollie olives are disciplined, but this is a garden full of life. Tucked within the formal structure are productive vegetable beds and an orchard of pomegranates, apples, peaches, pears, apricots, oranges, and figs.

When the Krehbiels moved in 2008, they immediately set to work on the hillside, which was inaccessible and unusable. They were inspired by Yaz's mother, who has a widely admired garden on Chicago's North Shore: "It's really a tribute to Posy. We learned so much from her. In our own small way, we knew how important it could be to have a warm and welcoming garden and how much it makes being outside with friends and family special." The Krehbiels hired designer Janell Denler Hobart, who recognized the possibilities of the sloping, south-facing site and designed paths that could access it in an inviting way. Hobart took out all the overgrowth down to bare earth, leaving a few existing trees—the oranges, a pepper tree, and the cypresses—and restored the hardscape of the weathered old walls, made of the same stone that was used to build the San Francisco Theological Seminary in San Anselmo. Close to the house, Denler Hobart created a structure of boxwood and olive shapes that are kept tightly clipped; this is in contrast to the imaginative vegetable and flower plantings further up the hillside.

As one would expect at the home of a landscape painter (Yaz), color is an important element here. In the spring, the parterres are full of Tulip Barcelona, which mirrors the deep raspberry color of the mature Vulcan magnolia at the entrance. White roses on the hillside are the foil for the ribbon of silvery licorice plants and the stone of the terrace. Pink erigerons have seeded

Above: The planting of *Hydrangea macrophylla* 'Alba' close to the house resonates with the silver foliage of the licorice plants along the wall.

Opposite: The clipped shapes of boxwood and 'Little Ollie' olives create a rhythm punctuated by the mature strawberry tree (*Arbutus unedo*) at the top of the stairs.

Overleaf: Gravel paths are threaded throughout the hillside, providing easy access to the vegetables, fruits, and flowers.

Above: White Meidiland roses bloom nonstop in the garden.

Opposite: Pink Pearl apple tree ready for harvesting.

themselves throughout. There are yellow accents as well—daffodils in the spring, David Austin Golden Celebration roses along the upper path, and lemon trees in pots on the terrace. Texture is also important: creeping wild rye, a drought-tolerant California native, has been planted as a soft understory to the orchard trees.

Since the three-quarter-acre property has no lawn, the chief playspaces for the children are the paths that loop through the hillside, making it very easy to pluck a cucumber for breakfast or a Pink Pearl apple for an afternoon snack. Growing things has definitely become part of the Krehbiels' family life. Different vegetables are planted every year, depending on the food that they might want to cook and experiment with. There is a family tradition of making peach puree every year and, with all the fruit that is grown on the property, there is plenty of jam- and applesauce-making in season as well.

TOM HANSEN AND
IRA HIRSCHFIELD GARDEN

MILL VALLEY

Perched at the top of a small steep lot and spread around a Mediterranean-style house, this walled, garden is made up of a series of narrow terraces overlooking Richardson Bay. The exuberantly planted entrance is a foretaste of the multi-faceted garden ahead, which provides all the impact, incident, and variety of a much larger place.

The bones of the garden were created eighteen years ago by landscape architect Steve Stucky. He enclosed the property with a high wall and designed a pathway around the house, a series of small ponds and waterfalls on the north side and terracing on the steep hill at the back, then installed it with Japanese maples, rhododendron, azaleas, and ferns. It is a different garden today.

Above: The street planting by the entrance gate consists of tough deerproof plants, including *Cistus landaniferus* 'Blanche' against the wall and chondropetalum, agave, and aeonium.

Opposite: Apricot 'Just Joey,' yellow 'Golden Celebration' and pink *Rosa mutabilis* thrive in the upper bed of the rose garden, as does a vigorous Meyer lemon. Spanish lavender and boxwood adorn the lower bed.

The turning point was a visit to Mexico. The drifts of aloes, the gray tones of elaeagnus, and the striking use of Italian cypress triggered an immediate understanding of what a climatically appropriate garden might look like. Shortly after the return to Northern California, the transformation of the garden began with the arrival of the first of what would be many Italian cypress, three six-foot plants that are now magnificent thirty-foot specimens. Over time, the Japanese maples and rhododendron have been replaced by olive and rosemary, palms, aeoniums, and agave.

Although this is a stroll garden, it was not designed for that purpose. The concept is rather as a series of distinct episodes, so paths will curve or a plant will obscure the next garden "event" and the garden unfolds in self-contained units linked by a common plant palette. The Japanese garden tradition of compression, then expansion, of space, of dark and then light are tools used to make the garden feel bigger than it is. Texture, form, and leaf color create the atmosphere—there are flowers but they are not the primary influence in the design. The plant palette is relatively restrained but playfully treated. Aeoniums, a particular favorite, might be used as a single focal point or, in a different setting, massed as a background.

On the garden tour, different moods are evoked, beginning with the sloping, shady path which, leads down by a gently burbling water feature to a small kitchen terrace and then through to a tiny garden shed, meant more for quiet reading and entertaining than storing tools. A circular stone terrace sits on wide stone stairs descending to a gently curved viewing terrace. This gracious, formal moment, aligned with the house, is the ceremonial centerpiece, marking a transition to the more informal elements on the lower level. The climb back up passes through another shady, narrow passageway to a wide and sunny terrace dominated by a magnificent Canary Island palm and a panoramic view of Richardson Bay.

Above: One of the original six cypresses provides a focal point for the lower walkway, which is edged with lavender. The water channel provides drainage for the hillside.

Opposite: A handsome pot set in a bed of aeonium, *Beschorneria albiflora*, orange-flowered leucospermum, and soft gray mounds of coastal rosemary (*Westringia fruticosa* 'Morning Light').

VILLA INSTEDA

RUTHERFORD

Chotsie Blank didn't consider herself a gardener when she and her husband, Allan, bought their house in the mid-1980s. But she knew she liked roses, and when she saw the house she imagined a garden that would be in keeping with the Victorian architecture, warm and old-fashioned. The Blanks felt fortunate in inheriting beautifully sited trees on the seven-acre property, including a massive sycamore and both a copper and a tri-color beech. Years after they'd moved in, they found out that the landscape architect Thomas Church planted them for previous owners. The trees anchor the grounds and give them an illusion of age and permanence, but, in fact, the landscape has gone through a series of changes over the last thirty years.

The romantic, rose-filled gardens are the result of highly effective partnerships: first, in 1988, with garden designer Sarah Hammond, who created a cottage-style rose garden for the back of the house, where there had originally been a pumpkin patch, with white picket fencing, pergolas, and arbors. Three years after they put in the first roses, the plants started to die and armillaria root rot (oak root fungus) was discovered in two huge walnut stumps underneath the garden. They excavated all the soil—including dynamiting out the stumps—and let the garden lie fallow for a year, but as soon as they started to plant and water again, the fungus returned. With the help of garden designer Roger Warner, they again removed all the soil and this time they also tried Allan Blank's idea of installing a swimming pool liner with drains. For double insurance, Warner, designed a raised brick plinth for the garden beds and Allan Blank designed twenty-four columns to provide vertical interest.

When Chotsie Blank originally envisioned the garden, she thought about two gardens that she greatly admired in France: La Roseraie de l'Hay, an historic "rose-only" garden, and the Bagatelle rose garden in the Bois de Boulogne in Paris. Her next partner on the property was the landscape designer and plantsman Gary Ratway of Digging Dog Nursery. Ratway used a procession

Above: An espaliered pomegranate grows on the wall of the shed, which was originally a root cellar and is now used for wine storage.

Opposite: Clipped edging of teucrium sets off the pillars of the apricot-colored climbing rose 'Polka' and the deep-pink rose 'Gertrude Jekyll.'

Two climbing roses, the blush-colored 'Eden' and the pink 'Cressida,' intertwine on the pillars in the central part of the garden.

ST. EDEN GARDEN

OAKVILLE

There is something dreamy about the St. Eden Garden. The quality of light under the ancient oaks, the muted colors, the soft rounded outlines of the shrubs and perennials, a sense of remove from the wider landscape all combine to create the mood of repose and beauty that have been the hallmark of this garden for almost three decades. Pam Kramlich has worked with many landscape professionals, and each has contributed here. But Kramlich herself, inspired by gardens of Provence, has a clear sense of the qualities she wants in her garden and has been able to preserve its rare atmosphere over the years.

The origins of the garden go back to 1943 when Baron Constantine Ramsay bought a parcel of red rocky soil near Oakville and created the Villa Mt. Eden Vineyard. Eden refers to the region's name on nineteenth-century maps. In 1989 art patrons Pam and Dick Kramlich bought Eden Rock, the eleven-acre vineyard, and the house on seven acres of wooded knoll adjacent to it. In addition to developing the vineyard, they hired landscape architect Jack Chandler to draw plans for a garden, and he laid out pathways and a swimming pool. The slightly elevated knoll overlooks miles of working vineyards, and from the swimming pool there is a clear view of Mount St. Helena. Chandler was followed by Sarah Hammond, who suggested the color scheme of grays, silvers, chartreuse, and purples and planted groups of lavender, teucrium, and hellebores.

Above and opposite: Oaks shade the house and the repetition of the soft gray mounds of olive 'Little Ollie' and teucrium provide a restful moment. The groundcover is *Erigeron karvinskianus.*

The designer Roger Warner took over from there and, working with the existing oak canopy, he expanded the garden, transforming it to the enchanted place it is today. Using plant form and placement for visual structure, and with a nod to the vineyards that surround the site, he sculpted lavender and teucrium balls, placing the lavender in rows radiating out to the edge of the garden, where they meet the neat rows of upright vines. He artfully inserted destinations: a gathering space for entertaining and performance; a simple lawn with rock outcroppings; a moon viewing lawn; "strawberry steps" for growing and eating

Above: A neighboring vine-yard can be seen through the oaks. Mounds of olive 'Little Ollie' are set against a band of *Hydrangea arborescens* 'Annabelle' backed by the feathery inflorescences of *Salvia turkestanica* 'alba.'

Opposite: In another clearing, groups of rocks are placed to look like natural outcroppings.

Overleaf: In autumn, the gray-green of olive 'Little Ollie' and the colorful tints of Cornus 'Eddie's White Wonder' are especially effective with the oaks.

fraise des bois; a quince allée. Skilled at creating mood, Warner enhanced the mid-story, planting forty Eddie's White Wonder dogwood that provide a layer of white bloom under the oaks in the spring and puffs of pinkish-orange color in the fall. He also added the chartreuse euphorbia blooms and more of the silvery rosemary, nepeta, salvias, and lavender, keeping to the simple plant palette that had evolved and repeating shapes and plants throughout the garden.

Other designers have contributed, beginning with a rose garden designed by Claudia Schmidt featuring soft pink, yellow, peach, white, and apricot roses on a terraced hillside behind the house. More recently, Silvina Blasen swapped out much of the lavender for the gray rounded form of the olive Little Ollie, as well as boxwood balls and mass plantings of blue fescue, true to the color scheme and emphasizing the perception of soft shapes floating beneath the gnarled forms of the oaks. Pam Kramlich's little bit of Provence continues to feel like a world apart, a respite from the hard light of the Napa sun that shines on the endless rows of vines glimpsed through the frame of the oaks.

RED WALNUT VINEYARD GARDEN

OAK KNOLL

Even before the 2012 drought, some Californians were actively looking to create gardens that would minimize water use, and they were making the aesthetic adjustments to see beauty in a drier environment that more directly conforms to the indigenous landscapes. Red Walnut Vineyard Garden was installed in 2010, but it clearly embraces principles of environmental responsibility that have now become a necessity rather than a choice.

The house and garden are set into a small vineyard. The land is flat, and the view stretches out in three directions across the valley floor. The owner's sister, a noted landscape architect and theoretician, recommended Ron Lutsko as a designer whose deep knowledge of California plants is matched by a refined contemporary sensibility. The brief was a garden that required minimum care, one that would enable the family to enjoy an indoor-outdoor lifestyle, have room for sports, and embrace the views.

Above: Concrete pavers set in gravel lead to the house. Olive trees are planted to the left and right and there is a large native valley oak at left.

Opposite: The back garden looks out to the Vaca Mountains. Blue Oat grass (*Helictotrichon sempervirens*) and Cleveland Sage (*Salvia clevelandii*) edge the concrete pad, which is shaded by an old walnut tree.

Lutsko, with project manager Andrea Kovol, gave them all that in an elegant design that depends on drought-tolerant plants and few simple materials. Key is replacing the traditional grass with a light tan-colored gravel and using concrete in several finishes for the edges and paving. Also crucial was to site the pool so it was not the main feature in the backyard but instead at the extreme western edge of the garden area, inserted directly into the vineyard.

In the central space around the house, a large concrete pad provides a place for comfortable seating and a dining area; the rest of the fenced garden is gravel. A Corten steel fire pit in the southeastern corner is backed by a seating wall at right angles to the one by the pool that directs the eye into the fields and then to the view of the Vaca Mountains beyond. The soft gray of olive trees planted on a grid acts as a backdrop to the living area and hides a sports court and a neighbor's house, ensuring that from the garden area one is only aware of the vineyard and the long views.

SKYHILL

Sue Bloch and Igor Khandros were East Coast transplants looking for a weekend retreat from high-pressure lives when they bought Skyhill, an eighty-acre ridge-top property, a decade ago. Skyhill held promise: there were magnificent views, a large pond, and some scraggly fields, but the land cried out for attention. The couple decided to start working on the landscape before taking on a house renovation. With no gardening experience but a growing understanding of what they wanted, they were searching for professional help when they were introduced to the work of John Greenlee with his "golden meadow" exhibition at the San Francisco Flower Show and immediately recognized an approach that they felt was right for their site.

Greenlee, nicknamed the guru of grass, is a passionate proselytizer for the beauty of meadows and the value of plant-based design. The couple found him an excellent listener and teacher and, after six months of discussion and preparation, work began on what would become five acres of gardens. Greenlee said that when his clients agreed to put in almost two miles of deer fence, he realized that this was going to be a serious endeavor. For the first two years, he worked intensively with them, creating an extensive meadow around the pond, and has remained involved even as the couple have gained confidence, built relationships with other experts, and spread their wings.

Above: The house sits in a meadow of pennisetum.

Opposite: A handcrafted wooden bridge spans the edge of the pond in front of a Japanese-inspired garden.

Overleaf: Restios, carpet roses, fescue, *verbena bonariensis*, and salvias mingle near the pond.

The initial effort was to get rid of what Greenlee calls the "disturbance ecology," the opportunistic plants that had moved in on the neglected landscape. Once weeds were eradicated, Greenlee planted hundreds of plugs of grasses, later adding perennials and trees. Nursery owner and aquatic plant expert Susan Golden was called in to help rejuvenate the pond. Although the different greens and golds of the grasses are predominant, now the landscape is a luxurious mixed planting, full of the vibrant color of roses and bright stands of garden favorites like verbena bonariensis and the more expected goldenrod all mixed together.

Above: The yellow fall color of the gingkos is set off by black pine (*Pinus thunbergii* 'Thundercloud') and a soft wave of *Pennisetum spathiolatum*.

Opposite: A maple pathway winds through the native madrones (*Arbutus menziesii*) and oaks. The maples include *Acer palmatum* 'Linearilobum' and *Acer palmatum* 'Seiryu.'

As they learned about plants, Bloch and Khandros developed their own passions—some, like the conifers, were introduced by Greenlee and some were motivated by travel and inclination. Bloch and Khandros had spent time in Japan, and there is a Japanese-influenced garden on the edge of the pond, but what really inspired them were Japanese maples. Igor Khandros collects enthusiastically: now there are probably 250 specimens planted on the property. Buying adventures to far-flung specialty nurseries have become the norm, a sure sign of garden obsession, and there are collections of ferns, bulbs, hellebores, fruit trees, and thirty of the showy sycamore maple Eskimo Sunset.

Whatever they collect, however many specimens they buy, fundamental for Sue Bloch is respecting the integrity of this particular place. Plants do not have to be native, but they must look at home—nothing goes in, no matter how wonderful it seemed at the nursery, if it doesn't look right in the property. Thus, restios, which are native to the southern hemisphere, are a favorite species here, their upright rush-like habit mimicking the grasses and fitting right into the general aesthetic.

RICHARD AND TATWINA
LEE GARDEN

CALISTOGA

This is a garden that has so melded into the natural landscape that the line between what has been planted and what was there before can barely be distinguished. The effect belies the enormous effort it took to make sure that, as Tatwina Lee explained, "the mountain [would be] allowed to take over again, but maybe with a sensitive hand." Landscape architects Eric and Silvina Blasen provided the sensitive hand, forming a deep relationship with the land and with the Lees, who wanted to be outside and close to nature but not responsible for a high-maintenance garden.

The house, designed by the Lees' son Eliot, a partner at Steven Harris Architects, and their daughter-in-law, Eun Sun Chun, is a series of rectilinear

Above: Tall concrete panels define the precinct of the house and garden.

Opposite: Narrow packed-dirt and concrete paths lead to the house and on into the garden.

Overleaf: Arctostaphylos 'Pacific Mist' surrounds the lawn plinth.

rammed-earth-and-concrete buildings spread along the ridge, with striking views on one side across the Napa Valley to the Mayacamas and Mount St. Helena; on the other, views of the Diamond Mountains provide the "magic" that captivated the family on their very first visit. Tall, eighteen-inch-thick concrete walls frame views and provide a much-needed windbreak. Ninety solar panels produce all their energy. The narrow, unobtrusive hiking path that leads from the parking area to the house sets the tone for the gardens beyond.

When planning the garden together, the challenge was to find appropriate plants that would survive the harsh conditions on the rocky hilltop. The architects and the Lees quickly settled on the idea of "what's wrong with what's already there" as a design principle. Diseased pines were replaced with the native scrub oak and blue oak, and four varieties of manzanita were planted in addition to already existing mature trees. Silvina Blasen experimented with several different varieties of ceanothus with little success—collecting seed, taking cuttings, cloning plants—but meanwhile, the native one from the mountain started to come in and it turned out to be bushy and low, just what they were looking for. Other native plants were added, including the shrub coffeeberry and the fragrant California snowdrop, which provides an

exceptional moment in spring when the blossoms fall, leaving a carpet of white on the ground. Succulents, hardy perennials, and annuals, especially salvias and poppies, add color and interest. It took a few years of intensive weeding to get the plants established, but now everything has knit together.

The raised-bed vegetable garden, tucked out of sight, was the Blasens' idea, but it has become a real part of the family's conversation with the land. The conditions are challenging, thanks to the wind, sun, and birds, but the Lees have learned how to succeed. Over the years, they've gotten advice from Napa Valley farmers, who, as Tatwina Lee says, "Don't like to tell you much but if they feel you're really trying, then once a year they'll give you one secret." Six secrets have been shared so far, perhaps the most important one being that everything needs shade when you're gardening on an exposed site at an elevation of nine hundred feet. A small orchard provides apples, peaches, nectarines, and pomegranates; on a typical weekend, the Lees might harvest two to three hundred pounds of produce to bring back to the city to grateful friends and colleagues.

Above: The utility table is used for cleaning and preparing the harvest and for serving meals in the vegetable garden.

Opposite above: The plantings effectively hide the separate garden spaces.

Opposite below: Arctostaphylos 'Emerald Carpet' and 'Pacific Mist' shelter the pool.

Above: A mix of *Salvia sonomensis* and *Salvia cleve-landii* 'Winifred Gilman' hold the hillside, and California native poppies have seeded themselves in the steps.

Opposite: The entrance opening frames a view of the Mayacamas Mountains.

Above: An allée of olive trees in front of an untitled sculpture by Donald Judd.

Opposite: Bougainvillea is clipped tight against the golden wall of the house.

Overleaf: A gnarled olive tree is juxtaposed with the dramatically sited *Serpentine* by Richard Serra.

Beyond the terrace is a hillside rose garden with flowers in every shade but red; the roses are interplanted with catmint to hide their leggy lower branches. Also behind the house is an impressive hillside of hydrangea that came about because white hydrangea is the potted plant of preference for decorating the interiors. When they have finished blooming, it is the gardener's practice to plant them on the hillside. Over the years the collection has multiplied. On a rise to the south, beyond the terrace, clouds of Russian sage, salvias, agastache, phlox, monarda, nicotiana, and geranium among others mingle in a naturalistic planting, which eventually blends into the hillside.

Although this is the home of one of America's great art collecting families, the garden and landscape are a magnificent example of the adage "less is more." In addition to the two works on the terrace, there is a Richard Serra beside a magnificent live oak at the foot of the hill, and that, along with the forty-five ancient olive trees, is the art displayed. No curator could do a better job.

Above: A dry stream meanders through unusual specimens of evergreens in many different forms.

Opposite above: The setting sun highlights the different colors and forms of this exceptional composition.

Opposite below: In the dry pond garden, carefully considered plant choices emphasize the textures of the different elements.

the paths are the centerpiece. The visitor is meant to walk through counter-clockwise so that the zig-zag plank bridge with its plantings of calla lilies and Japanese iris is crossed facing the house. Creeping juniper follows the contours of the land and trees are used as punctuation points. As in traditional stroll gardens, there are several vantage points along the way that make the most of the changes in elevation.

The Brandwenes have willingly embraced the challenge of keeping the garden up to the level that they imagine the Hasegawas would have expected. They have studied old photographs and replanted within the original plant palette, even though, as in the case of heaths and heathers, some of those plants are difficult to come by and maintain. They prune to keep the shapes in control and carefully set the irrigation so that the mostly drought-tolerant garden will get the water it needs but no more. The garden is not frozen in time. It changes subtly with the seasons and years, and the guiding spirit of Noriko Hasegawa continues to echo in this remarkable landscape.

THE MELISSA GARDEN

HEALDSBURG

Barbara and Jacques Schlumberger's garden wasn't always called the Melissa Garden. For the first five years they lived on the forty-acre property, the focus was on the house, adjacent pool, and the large vegetable garden and orchard. Barbara was already a beekeeper, and in 2006, when she heard about colony collapse disorder and the precipitous decline nationwide in honeybee populations, she wanted to do more. She enlisted the advice of fellow beekeepers Priscilla Coe and Michael Thiele in creating a sanctuary that could protect the bees as well as other important pollinators. The name Melissa means honeybee in Greek. In mythology it is also the name of the nymph who cared for Zeus as a baby, sustaining him with watered-down honey. Kate Frey, the longtime garden designer at Fetzer Vineyards and gold medal winner at the Chelsea Flower Show, was charged with designing a garden whose main measure of success would not be the coherence of color, texture, and form, but instead the number of pollinators that would be attracted and their ability to thrive.

Above: A beehive, almost engulfed by a planting of cleome, bidens, *Salvia uliginosa*, calamint, nepeta, Sedum 'Autumn Joy,' and a few pink cosmos.

Opposite: A melange of sunflowers, cosmos, gaillardia, bidens, and Salvia 'Mystic Spires.'

A square vegetable garden was transformed into a roughly circular flower garden, with criss-crossing paths and a fountain in the center. The serpentine clay soil was enriched with loads of compost made from cow manure and green waste and, thanks to the soil preparation, the garden grew quickly to an abundant eden. The goal was to have something in bloom as much of the year as possible, and the list of bee-friendly plants originally included over one hundred species balanced between California natives, like coffeeberry and blue tansy, and Mediterranean plants. In February or March, the poppies and blue tansy begin their long bloom periods. By May and June, the garden is at its peak with a riot of color, including plants like catmint, calamintha, milkweed, salvias, agastache, Russian sage, and lavender, followed by sunflowers and cleome in the summer. Bees need a certain area of each plant's bloom to forage so plants are set out in three-by-three-foot blocks or the same plant is repeated in the garden. The effect is of a wildly busy landscape, with bees, butterflies, birds, and moths flitting around everywhere.

Above: *Echium candicans,* Lemon balm, *Agastache foeniculum,* and Dusty Miller are among the plants selected for their "attractive" qualities.

Opposite: Bees are particularly drawn to the vibrant colors of Agastache 'Kudos Coral,' Agastache 'Tutti Frutti,' *Verbena bonariensis, Solidago rugosa,* and a selection of the native mimulus.

Over the years, the garden has flourished. An orchard of pomegranates, figs, apricots, and persimmons was seeded with blue tansy, creating an understory of soft blue. Maintenance has consisted mostly of encouraging the beneficial plants and keeping out the thugs like annual echium and evening primrose, which are exiled to the outer perimeters of the garden. The garden is entirely organic, with compost added yearly as a mulch for soil fertility. Even so, constant cutting back and deadheading is essential for keeping the garden in shape and bloom. The garden was open to the public for almost eight years, and hundreds of visitors came every year to study the pollinators and admire the plantings. Now that it has reverted to a private property, the gardens continue to be a source for both sustenance and beauty.

HOG HILL

SEBASTOPOL

Mary Reid is at heart a painter and Lew Reid is passionate about plants. That turns out to be a superb combination for garden making. The Reids found their property, now 140 acres, on a remote hilltop in Sebastopol in 1989 after a long search and began the fruitful collaboration that resulted in this extraordinary garden. Although already a garden designer, when faced with the responsibility of creating a garden in this spectacular site with its wide-open views of high rolling pasture and wooded mountains, Mary Reid took herself to England for six weeks to study with the noted designer and teacher John Brookes and also at Kew Gardens. She came back and spent the winter developing a plan that has served them well ever since. Meanwhile, she and her husband prepared a wish list of their favorite plants and put up a temporary greenhouse where he began to propagate the hundreds of plants they would need for the two acres they planned for a garden.

Above: Taller plants like the pomegranate (*Punica* 'La Grill') frame the view, and mounding shrubs and perennials, including roses, sedum 'Autumn Joy,' *Salix purpurea* 'Nana,' and *Berberis thunbergii* 'Gold Ring' lead the eye gently into the distance.

Opposite: The skillful use of color holds these disparate components together. The dark red of cotinus 'Grace' is picked up by eucomis 'Smoking Burgundy' and echoed by leucadendron 'Safari Sunset'. The shape of the eucomis also relates to the spiky forms of *Agave americana* var. *mediopicta* 'Alba.'

Mary Reid's challenge as a designer was to fit the view and the garden in the same frame in ways that did not detract from either. The couple built a simple craftsman-style house, and the twenty-four-foot span of the interior courtyard became the view corridor to the land that sloped to the south. At a short distance from the house, she installed a retaining wall, where she could grow plants up to six feet tall on the lower side without impinging on the long view that gave the property its appeal. The trees were grouped on the edges of that central viewing corridor, a strong system of pathways was established, and the complex and highly textured garden became the magnificent foreground.

Once the structure was in place, she focused on texture, foliage, and finding plants with staying power, because in such a large, organically grown garden featuring big sweeps of plants there is no room for a plant that does not pull its weight for most of the year. The Reids were drawn to Mediterranean plants although not exclusively; there are also a number of specimens of Asian origin, and Lew Reid has a collection of more than one hundred maples. Armed with an

import license, they also traveled to places like Australia and South Africa and came back with cuttings and seeds that he would turn into full-grown plants.

But more than the sum of the many precious individual specimens in this garden, it is the sense of color in the composition that sets it apart. When asked if color is important to her, Mary Reid is surprised, "Well, of course, that's how I organized my garden, the blue bed, the gray bed. Otherwise, it would have been too difficult to deal with such a big space." While she uses a wide range of colors, there are certain tones that tie the composition together, like chartreuse, which makes other colors pop when displayed against it, and the silvery grays of the lavenders. The red-leaved trees and shrubs, from the four different cultivars of the smoke bush to the red berberis to the reds of numerous Japanese maples, provide vivid counterpoints.

Gardens are never static and a great deal of maintenance goes into this garden. To those who have been lucky enough to visit, it seems a finished work of art. But Lew Reid is still acquiring interesting specimens, and Mary Reid has moved from full-time painting with plants to a new career painting with watercolors, inspired no doubt by what she has learned from so many years perfecting her vast and beautiful canvas.

Above: Mounding forms of pennisetum 'Hameln' echo the larger *Melianthus major* behind.

Opposite: A strong path system provides structure for the billowing perennials while mature trees and tall shrubs create complex garden walls. The dark purple-hued cotinus 'Grace' contrasts with the bright-toned variegated *Cornus kousa* 'Cherokee Sunset.'

251

Left: Ceramic sculpture by Charlie Washburn gives a focal point to the large sweeps of perennials and grasses.

Overleaf: Chartreuse is used throughout to unite disparate elements. The fall color of the Japanese maple (*Acer palmatum* 'Fjellheim') on the left echoes the glowing mound of spiraea 'Ogon.' The tall form of the golden locust (*Robinia pseudoacacacia* 'Frisia') repeats the tint, as do the lime flowers of Siberian spurge (*Euphorbia seguieriana* ssp. *niciciana*) lining the path.

ACKNOWLEDGMENTS

We would like to thank our editor and part-time Bay Area resident, Elizabeth White, for once again sending us off on a great adventure, and our designer, Susan Evans, for joining Elizabeth to put it all together so beautifully.

A project like this depends entirely on the generosity of all the gardeners who shared their insights and gardens with us. We are enormously grateful for the kindness we met right across the Bay Area, and for the time so many took to show us their fabulous gardens. These gardens and gardeners provided our education and this book would not have been possible without them.

A big thank you to the stewards of the Bay Area's public gardens who were particularly generous, including Christina Syrett and Beth Lau at Filoli and the indomitable Shelagh Fritz at Alcatraz, as well as Antonia Adezio at the Marin Art & Garden Center. We also spent two delightful and educational afternoons with Walker Young and Ryan Penn at the Ruth Bancroft Garden.

To former employees of the Garden Conservancy, Diane Botnick, Laura Palmer and Laura Wilson, thank you. It would have been so much harder to prepare this book without your detailed knowledge of the gardens in the Bay Area. And to Antonia Hunter and Elizabeth Everdell from the Board of The Garden Conservancy, your advice, guidance and collegiality over the past two years has been as enjoyable as it was invaluable. To Pam Kramlich, longstanding friend and patron, we owe our valuable introduction to the wine country. Also to Sisi and Bert Damner, thank you for help, advice, and encouragement along the way.

We have been fortunate to have met and learned from many of the outstanding professionals working in the Bay Area, both in the design and nursery fields. They have been unstinting with their time and their ideas and without exception we have enjoyed and profited by our interactions with them. It is a long list to thank and includes Silvina and Eric Blasen, Todd Cole, Kate Frey, John Greenlee, Virginia Harmon, Annie Hayes, James Lord and Roderick Wylie, Ron Lutsko, Timothy Szybalski, Bernard Trainor, Dick Turner, and Brandon Tyson.

Thanks to Caitlin Atkinson for valuable tips and years of support. Thanks also go to Murrayl Berner for finding us food and shelter and entertaining us at the end of long days, and to Robert Shimshak for being such a good sport and letting us share Marion for the last two and a half years. And, finally, to all those whose gardens appear in these pages, this is your book as well as ours. We are deeply grateful for the time you took with us, answering our many questions and touring us around your gardens. Any problems or errors are of course ours, the glorious gardens are yours and we thank you for them.